THE ISLAMIC STATE

Terror in the Name of Religion

Written by Benoît Lefèvre
Translated by Rebecca Neal

History 50MINUTES.com

THE ISLAMIC STATE

KEY INFORMATION

- **Year founded:** 2006, during the Mujahideen Shura Council in Iraq, which brought together five jihadist groups and around 30 Sunni tribes. The terrorist group proclaimed the Islamic State of Iraq in October 2006, before becoming the Islamic State of Iraq and the Levant in 2013.
- **Ideology:** Salafi jihadism (Sunni Islam).
- **Founders:**
  - Abu Musab al-Zarqawi (1966-2006)
  - Abu Omar al-Baghdadi (died in 2010)
  - Abu Bakr al-Baghdadi (born in 1971).
- **Names:** *al-Dawlah al-Islamīyah fī al-'Irāq wa-al-Shām*, meaning Islamic State of Iraq and the Levant (ISIL) in English, Islamic State of Iraq and Syria (ISIS), the Islamic State, or Daesh (Arabic acronym for ISIL, which is considered to be pejorative by members of the terrorist cell). Others prefer to refer to it as the so-called, self-proclaimed or self-styled Islamic State as a way of signalling their refusal to consider the terrorist group as a true state.
- **Objectives:**
  - to found a caliphate bringing together the entire Muslim world, on the model of the Abbasid Caliphate;
  - to fight against the West, which it considers responsible for the persecution of Muslims over the centuries;
  - to fight against Shia Muslims.

INTRODUCTION

In January 2015, the satirical newspaper *Charlie Hebdo* was targeted by terrorists, along with a Jewish supermarket, where an armed man took staff and customers hostage. The death toll was high: 17 people were killed during the attacks. On 13 November of the same year, the French capital was once again hit by a series of attacks which claimed 130 victims, who were shot down in the street, in cafés or in the Bataclan theatre. On 22 March 2016, Belgium fell victim to multiple suicide attacks, when bombs were set of at Brussels airport and the Maelbeek metro station, a short distance from the European institutions, leaving 32 dead and over 200 wounded. These are just two examples among many: the USA, Iraq, Syria, Egypt and Turkey have also been hit by attacks.

These attacks were claimed by an organisation which was until then largely unknown to the general public, and which goes by the name of the Islamic State or ISIS. This relatively young, but no less powerful, organisation claims to be aligned with Islam and is driven by the desire to wage jihad against all of Western civilisation, as well as by its intention to restore the Abbasid Caliphate, which fell in 1258. The group was founded in 2006 and developed in a specific historical context, namely the war in Iraq and Syria, which favoured the rapid rise of armed extremism, spread by men nostalgic for the former power of the Muslim world.

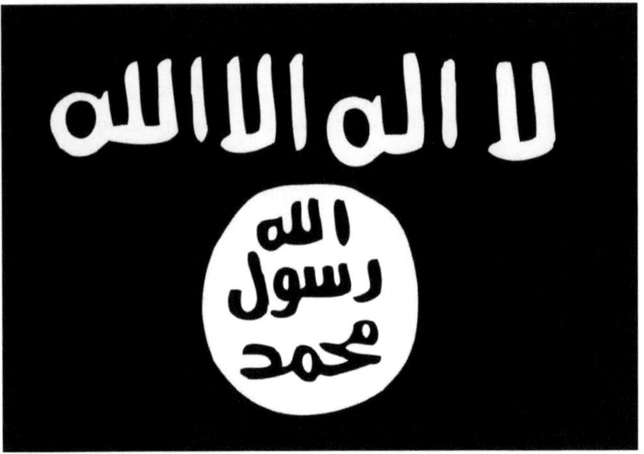

The flag of the Islamic State.

JIHAD

The concept of jihad was formulated after the death of Muhammad (570-632) by Muslim religious scholars. Originally meaning 'struggle', the term refers to the war effort against non-Muslims. It was decreed by the caliph himself, the head of the Ummah (the Muslim community throughout the world), or by one of his representatives. Although jihad has not been officially proclaimed since 1914, it is regularly taken up by groups of independent fighters who give it a warlike meaning. They use it to evoke a sort of anti-Crusade against the West and the fight against colonialism. This fight is waged while threatening Western culture and interests in the Middle East, which they claim corrupt the

Muslim elites.

From the 10th century onwards, some authors have developed a more moderate view of the concept by considering jihad as a defensive fight. Sufis (members of a Muslim mystical order) often distinguish between greater and lesser jihad. Greater jihad refers to the daily combat that each Muslim must wage against the temptations around them which could lead them to stray from the right path; in theory, therefore, it is not violent.

Although the Islamic State often makes the headlines, the general public tend to have a poor understanding of it. The group raises many questions: what is really hiding behind the Islamic State? How was it created? How does it work? What are its pressure tactics? All these questions will be answered in this guide.

THE ORIGINS OF THE ISLAMIC STATE

THE HISTORY OF IRAQ

An unstable country

The origins of the Islamic State are inextricably linked to the history of Iraq. The country was at one time the centre of the Arab world, but it became a British colony after the First World War (1914-1918) and only gained its independence in the second half of the 20th century, following a coup d'état by General Abd al-Karim Qasim (1914-1963) in July 1958. After the execution of the former leader of the country, King Faisal II (1883-1933), and those around him, the Republic of Iraq was proclaimed. It was led by the Ba'ath Party.

THE BA'ATH PARTY

The Ba'ath (literally 'resurrection') Party is an Arab nationalist political party in the Middle East. Its aim is to achieve Arab unification and to promote the economic, political and cultural independence of the Arab world. From 1950 onwards, socialist tendencies were added to this desire, resulting in a revitalisation of society.

The Ba'ath Party has been present in Iraq since 1949. After a long period operating underground, it officially became a prominent part of the political scene after the revolution in 1958, and firmly established its power ten years later.

In Syria, the Ba'ath Party came to power in the early 1960s and embarked on a policy of nationalisation. Hafez al-Assad (1930-2000), the father of Bashar al-Assad (President of Syria, born in 1965) was Secretary General of the party from 1970 onwards, before beco-ming president of the country the following year.

The al-Assad family: Hafez al-Assad and his wife (seated); behind him are his children, including Bashar al-Assad (second from left).

In 1968, Iraq was shaken by another coup d'état, resulting in the overthrow of the president Abdul Rahman Arif (1916-2007) and the restoration to power of the Ba'ath Party, which had been removed several years earlier. Ahmed Hassan al-Bakr (1914-1982) then became the leader of Iraq, assisted by his vice president Saddam Hussein (1937-2006).

Saddam's power increased over time, and before long he took advantage of the president's advanced age to seize the reins of power, before officially succeeding him in 1979. He then embarked on a series of purges, in particular within his party, which led to the deaths of hundreds of people.

Following the Islamic Revolution in Iran, Saddam led Iraq into a bloody and destructive war against its neighbour, which lasted for eight years and brought the country to its knees. He then attacked Kuwait, aiming in particular to increase his oil reserves, but once again his venture ended in failure. The UN punished him with an embargo on oil from Iraq, which was the country's main financial resource.

In spite of the disastrous state his country was in and the poverty faced by the Iraqi people, Saddam not only managed to maintain his power, but even strengthened it through a system of cronyism and by portraying himself as a bulwark against Western imperialism. The country was torn apart as it was beset by internecine wars and had to deal with high levels of criminality and corruption.

Photograph of Saddam Hussein.

A country split between several religions

Iraq is characterised by a very high degree of religious and ethnic diversity (Arabs, Kurds, Assyrians and Armenians, among others). The vast majority of the population is

Muslim (95%), but there are also Christians, Yazidis and Mandaeans.

The Muslim community, which makes up the vast majority of the population, is itself divided into two groups: the Shias, representing 65% of the country's Muslims, and the Sunnis, who make up the remaining 35%. These two groups originally belonged to a unified Islam but split after the death of the Prophet Muhammad, when it was time to choose a successor. While some (those who would become Shias) chose Ali, the Prophet's son-in-law, others (the future Sunnis) lent their support to Abu Bakr, his companion and father-in-law. In addition, the two groups did not share the same view of the role of the imam. While Sunnis saw him as one man among others who guided believers, for Shias he was a descendent of the Prophet who drew his power from God. This had political consequences, as Sunnis accepted the mixing of religion and politics, whereas Shias wanted to distinguish between the two. The Iraqi state apparatus has always been dominated by Sunnis, who are a minority in the country, with the Shias constantly subjugated.

RULE BY THE MINORITY IN IRAQ

One of the reasons Sunnis are in charge in Iraq is historic. In the time of the Ottoman Empire, the caliph was a Sunni, so his community was favoured. The Shias then formed a poorer rural community. When Iraq became a British colony, the Sunnis, who controlled the majority of the administration, were able to maintain their position. The Shias, on the other hand, chose to reject the colonialist presence and distanced themselves from politics.

Immediately after the end of the First Gulf War, which was triggered by Iraq's invasion of Kuwait, the country had to deal with uprisings in some majority-Shia regions. The rebellion was repressed so violently that the UN decided to intervene and created no-fly zones with the aim of protecting the population. The situation was catastrophic, especially as the USA was bombing Iraq on an almost daily basis in the late 1990s. However, Saddam managed to hold onto his position as leader of Iraq.

Rising violence

In 2003, the USA decided to invade Iraq, claiming that there were weapons of mass destruction in the country and that Saddam had links with terrorist groups, including al-Qaeda. The USA was supported in its mission by British troops. They invaded the country on 19 March and toppled the regime a few weeks later. Shortly afterwards, the UN Security Council handed over control of Iraq to the American and British coalition, so that it could embark on the process of rebuilding and restoring peace to the country. In September, a provisional government was put in place, but there was little improvement in the situation, and the American and British troops often faced open hostility.

In March 2004, the Shia Ayad Allawi (born in 1944) was appointed Interim Prime Minister, while the Sunni Ghazi Mashal Ajil al-Yawer (born in 1958) was chosen as President of Iraq. However, shortly afterwards, the guerrilla war between Sunnis and Shias resumed, resulting in destruction and bloodshed across the country. The Americans attempted to violently repress the fighting.

Photograph taken in 2004 in Fallujah, a city in central Iraq which became the scene of a series of violent clashes.

Elections were held in January 2005; as many Sunnis refused to participate, they were won by Shia candidates backed by Ayatollah Sistani (born in 1930). After extensive negotiations, the Kurdish politician Jalal Talabani (born in 1933) was chosen as President, with the Sunni Ghazi Mashal Ajil al-Yawer and the Shia Adil Abdul-Mahdi (born in 1942) as Vice Presidents. Immediately afterwards, a new constitution was drafted, but instead of improving the situation, it exacerbated the differences between the religious communities. The actions of the United States, which was not used to this kind of situation, also played a part in worsening it. Further elections were held at the end of the year. After lengthy talks, Talabani kept his position and the Shia Nouri al-Maliki (born in 1950) became Prime Minister. A few months later, al-Maliki unveiled a government of national unity tasked with re-establishing order. However, the violence did not lessen, and the USA decided to retake control of the situation. They launched a series of operations in order to put an end to the insurrections.

In 2008, an agreement for the withdrawal of foreign troops was signed. This withdrawal was slated to begin in June 2009 and be completed by December 2011. Further elections were held on 7 March 2010 in order to ensure a successful transition. Talabani and al-Maliki kept their posts.

After nine years of occupation, the last American troops left Iraq on 18 December 2011, leaving the country alone to build its future. The death toll of the operation was catastrophic: while the USA had lost over 4000 soldiers, over 110 000 Iraqis had been killed. In addition, George W. Bush (president of the USA, born in 1946) had waged an extensive campaign of de-Ba'athification by eliminating members of Saddam's party. There was a very large number of these, because many Iraqis had joined the party in the 1990s in order to become civil servants, without having any real affinity for the dictator and his ideas.

In spite of the withdrawal of foreign troops, tensions remained high and provided a breeding ground for terrorist groups such as the Islamic State. These radical groups took advantage of the extremely tense atmosphere to sow divisions within Iraqi society, stirring up hatred among Sunnis towards Shias and the West. They accused the USA of having occupied Iraqi territory, and more broadly the entire Middle East, for decades in order to exploit oil reserves in the Gulf. The sense of bitterness was exacerbated by the fact that promises to establish democracy had never been fulfilled. Salafists (members of a fundamentalist branch of Sunni Islam advocating a return to the text of the Qur'an) portrayed the Sunnis as victims, offered them a plan to emerge from their isolation and called for the violent overthrow of Shia power, which was presented as illegitimate and a deviation from true Islam. Consequently, on 15 October 2006, Iraqi insurgents formed an alliance and proclaimed the Islamic State of Iraq (*Dawlat al-ʿIrāq al-ʾIslāmiyyah*).

THE FOUNDERS OF THE ISLAMIC STATE

Abu Musab al-Zarqawi and the development of an armed group in Iraq

The Jordanian Abu Musab al-Zarqawi presented himself as the leader of this jihad against not only the West, but also against the Shias, who he hated more than anything else. He pledged allegiance to al-Qaeda in October 2004 and became the leader of the Iraqi branch of the organisation. He grouped together a number of Sunni factions around him.

Al-Zarqawi, originally called Ahmad Fadeel al-Nazal al-Khalayleh, was born in a working-class neighbourhood of Zarqa, a poor town in Jordan. His early life was turbulent and marked by a series of petty crimes. His mother was worried by his behaviour and decided to send him to a Qur'anic school, from which he emerged a changed man. Shortly afterwards, he decided to go to Afghanistan to fight against the Soviet Union, and adopted the new name Abu Musab al-Zarqawi.

After the departure of Soviet forces in 1989, the young

fighter chose to remain in Afghanistan, where he met Abu Muhammad al-Maqdisi. Al-Maqdisi wanted to overthrow the Arab governments that he viewed as corrupt, with the goal of changing society. The two men went to Jordan together to set up a terrorist cell there, but they were arrested and sentenced to 15 years in prison. This was when al-Zarqawi absorbed the ideas of Salafism. He left prison before the end of his sentence and returned to Afghanistan.

In 2000, he met Osama Bin Laden (1957-2011) for the first time in Kandahar, Afghanistan. He turned down his suggestion to join al-Qaeda, preferring instead to focus his efforts on the establishment of an Islamic state in the Middle East. He also led a training camp in Herat, Afghanistan, in order to prepare for suicide attacks in the Middle East. However, he was forced to leave Kandahar after American forces arrived in 2001.

After becoming leader of the jihadist group Jama'at al-Tawhid wal-Jihad, he organised several attacks in Iraq in 2003. The following year, Bin Laden incorporated al-Zarqawi's group into al-Qaeda, and it became known as al-Qaeda in Iraq. Thanks to this merging, al-Zarqawi was able to gather enough supporters and resources to fight against the American troops and launch a wave of suicide attacks in Iraq, bringing the country to the brink of civil war. However, his death following an American air strike in 2006 sowed discord in his organisation and left it divided over the question of his succession. Abu Omar al-Baghdadi ultimately assumed the leadership of the group.

The UN headquarters in Baghdad after a truck bombing in August 2013.

Abu Omar al-Baghdadi and the assertion of a group of fighters

Abu Omar al-Baghdadi was born to a Sunni family and claimed to be a descendant of the Prophet Muhammad.

His past remains mysterious, but many sources claim that he joined al-Qaeda in the mid-1980s. In 1999, he left Iraq for Afghanistan, where he became close to al-Zarqawi. After spending time in Kurdistan in 2002, he joined Jama'at al-Tawhid wal-Jihad the following year and officially announced his return to Iraq in 2004. He took part in the First Battle of Fallujah in April 2004 and the Second Battle of Fallujah in November 2004, in which American soldiers fought against Sunni insurgents. In particular, he oversaw the taking of hostages. Al-Baghdadi wrote about his profound hatred of Shias and Americans in a series of propaganda essays, in which he expounded his reasons for fighting and condemned those he viewed as apostates.

His role at Fallujah and his knowledge of the Qur'an allowed him to be named emir (governor) of the new Islamic State of Iraq in 2006. This state was founded on 15 October by the fringes of the Mujahideen Shura Council established by the Iraqi branch of al-Qaeda. However, the international community was not overly wary of al-Baghdadi, who they viewed as no more than a puppet for al-Zarqawi.

Al-Baghdadi died in April 2010 during a joint Iraqi-American operation. Under his leadership, the Islamic State drastically changed its strategy. Instead of focusing on an armed struggle against the USA and its allies, al-Baghdadi targeted Shias and, by extension, Iran (the leading majority-Shia country). This shift marked an initial distancing of the Islamic State from al-Qaeda.

Abu Bakr al-Baghdadi and the move towards the foundation of a caliphate

It was not until Abu Bakr al-Baghdadi assumed leadership of the group in 2010 that stability returned and the movement experienced real growth. The new strongman of the Salafist movement shifted even further away from al-Qaeda, and gave al-Qaeda in Iraq back the name Islamic State in Iraq.

Al-Baghdadi, who was probably born in Samarra, Iraq in 1971 and was originally called Awwad Ibrahim Ali Muhammad al-Badri al-Samarrai, also claims to be a direct descendent of the Prophet Muhammad. According to the jihadists, his family was very devout. His brothers and uncles reportedly include imams and professors of Arabic language, logic and rhetoric, while al-Baghdadi himself obtained a doctorate in Islamic Studies at the University of Baghdad before serving as an imam in the capital and in Fallujah.

During the American invasion in 2003, he joined the group led by al-Zarqawi, who he was quite close to. In 2005, he was captured and imprisoned by the occupying forces. After his release in 2009, he became emir of Rawa, a town close to the Syrian border, and presided over a sharia court. He stood out because of his brutality towards those accused of assisting the international coalition forces, who he had publicly executed.

In May 2010, he assumed leadership of the group. As he shared al-Zarqawi's conviction that a large, solid territorial base in the Middle East was essential to achieve his aims, he embarked on a traditional war in which he tried to conquer regions and towns and impose sharia (Islamic law) there. At the same time, he refused to pledge allegiance to al-Qaeda.

He took advantage of the conflict in Syria to extend the influence of his organisation, and sent armed men to fight against Bashar al-Assad's regime. For this reason, in 2013 the group took the name Islamic State of Iraq and the Levant.

On 29 June 2014, a few days after the capture of Mosul, the second-largest city in Iraq, he stood in the great mosque of the city and announced the restoration of the caliphate, of which he proclaimed himself leader. Since then, he has publicly demanded that all Muslims submit to his authority.

The caliph

The term 'caliph' comes from the Arabic word *khalīfa* and refers to a successor of Muhammad who leads the community of believers. Originally, the person named caliph held absolute power on Earth, conferred on him by Allah, and Muslims were completely under his authority.

During the second half of the 7th century, the Umayyad dynasty in Damascus held power in the caliphate. It was overthrown in the middle of the following century by the Abbasids, who made Baghdad their capital. Following a split in the 10th century, other caliphates emerged, in particular in Córdoba and Cairo. The last caliphate was abolished in 1924.

IDEOLOGY

RELIGIOUS STANCE

In terms of ideology, ISIL is part of Salafism, a branch of Sunni Islam which developed in the Arabian Peninsula. Salafism can cover a range of beliefs, but the groups which identify with this branch of Islam all share the desire to return to the roots of Islam, meaning the religion as it was practised by the *salaf* ("devout ancestors"), with the aim of resolving the problems in Muslim society. To rediscover what they consider the golden age of their religion, Salafists advocate a return to the text of the Qur'an, in order to purify Islam of the distinctive features that have been added to it over the centuries and have, in their eyes, falsified the divine message.

Salafist ideology owes a great deal to two figures. The first of these, Ahmad Ibn Hanbal was a 9th-century Mesopotamian theologian who opposed all forms of innovation and, more generally, philosophy, as this could lead believers to question the Salafist dogma that the rules of life have been imposed by God and passed on to the Prophet. In 1744, one of his disciples, Muhammad ibn Abd al-Wahhab, formed an alliance with Muhammad bin Saud, the leader of a tribe in the Arabian Peninsula, in order to unify the Arab tribes. This alliance culminated in the foundation of the Kingdom of Saudi Arabia in 1932 by the Saud dynasty, and had the effect of imposing Salafism across the entire peninsula.

Today, Salafism can be divided into three branches which

propose different ways of achieving its objective set:

- **quietist Salafism**, which promotes a re-Islamisation of Muslim societies through education, by returning to the religion as it was passed on by the Prophet;
- **revolutionary (or jihadist) Salafism**, which ISIL is part of, and which advocates armed jihad against non-Salafis and the establishment of an Islamic state;
- **political Salafism**, which transmits a militant vision of Islam.

AIMS

The restoration of the Abbasid Caliphate

Since the 1950s, Islamists and Islamic scholars have been promising the restoration of the original caliphate, the Sunni caliphate led by the Abbasids with Baghdad as its capital. This is portrayed as a perfect society, is seen by jihadists as the golden age of Islam. However, no Salafist leader, not even Osama Bin Laden, has been able to make this aim a reality, and, according to the jihadists, Muslims have gradually strayed from the right path.

THE ABBASID CALIPHATE

Thanks to the support of a movement that was hostile to the Umayyads, As-Saffah (721/722-754), the descendent of an uncle of Muhammad, was proclaimed caliph in 749. He then defeated the Umayyads at the Battle of the Zab in January 750 and assumed the leadership of a vast empire stretching from the Atlantic to the Indus River in South Asia. His successor moved the former Umayyad capital from Damascus to Baghdad, which was founded in 762. The caliphate reached its zenith under the reign of Harun al-Rashid (766-809) between 786 and 809. Its territory stretched from the coasts of Maghreb to the outskirts of Tripoli, and in the South of the Middle East from the Arabian Peninsula to the Southern Caucasus. However, its influence reached well beyond its borders and could be felt as far away as modern-day Morocco and Kashmir. The wealth of the towns and cities founded by the first Abbasids is evidence of the power of the caliphate. Its society was very heterogenous and organised according to a strict hierarchy. Non-Muslims, especially Jews and Christians, faced segregation. On the intellectual and religious level, traditionalist Sunni thought developed, as did a range of sciences, including mathematics, medicine, astronomy and geography.

However, the caliphate gradually faced increasing competition from different territories which seceded from it. These included the Caliphate of Córdoba (929-1031), which developed from an emirate founded on the Iberian Peninsula by Abd-ar-Rahman (731-788), the only survivor of the Umayyad dynasty, and the Fatimid Caliphate in Maghreb then Egypt (909-1171). In the 9th century, the Abbasid Caliphate was also weakened internally, in particular due to the influence of Turkish mercenaries on the caliphs.

Alongside this desire to restore a system which marked the zenith of Islam, Abu Bakr al-Baghdadi is also convinced that the borders which currently demarcate the Muslim world must be erased. He views these borders, which were drawn up after the First World War by the French and the British, as symbols of European colonialism and the cause of their decline. In short, Islamic State propaganda shows that the caliphate claims to be for Muslims what Israel is for Jews: a territory which brings together a religious community (in this case, the entire Muslim community, persecuted for centuries by the West) in the place where the faith originated (present-day Iraq and Syria). Al-Baghdadi rejects anything that could stand in the way of his project to restore the caliphate, such as democracy, secularism and nationalism.

The fight against the West and Shia Muslims

ISIL considers the West as an enemy that must be defeated, because it views it as the cause of all the ills that have befallen Iraq and Syria. The Western presence, first in colonies and then in the influence over and occupation of territories, has given rise to a profound feeling of humiliation.

It is also necessary to bear in mind the differences between the two ways of life. While Salafism promotes a traditional lifestyle in accordance with very strict rules which place religion and faith at the centre of the believer's existence, the European and American way of life is constantly developing and always looks towards the future. Western civilisation is the result of the Enlightenment and has undergone a phase of far-reaching secularisation, which has led to a very clear separation between Church and state and the promotion of individual freedoms. The most convinced Salafists, who base their ideas on a very radical reading of the Qur'an, view these freedoms as a form of extremism which threatens their society and even insults their religion. The attacks carried out in Paris in 2015 are a clear demonstration of this. The satirical newspaper *Charlie Hebdo* was attacked in response to the publication, permitted by the right to freedom of expression, of caricatures of the Prophet Muhammad, since any illustration of the Prophet is considered to be an insult to Islam. The attack on the Bataclan on 13 November targeted a concert by Eagles of Death Metal, a rock group which uses satanic imagery, while the killings in Parisian restaurants and cafés constituted a direct attack on the 'French way of life'.

Sacred iconography in Islam

Islam teaches that God cannot be represented, because He cannot be summed up in a single image. The issue of representations of Muhammad gives rise to further debates. While some, especially within Sunni communities, think that this ban also extends to the Prophet, others believe that Muhammad is a man like any other and can therefore be depicted. This is why there are many depictions of Muhammad in the Shia world.

The Islamic State aims to strike its enemies as they are going about their day-to-day lives, in places where there are many people. There are a number of reasons for this tactic. First of all, this strategy has proved to be very effective: setting off a bomb in the middle of a crowd guarantees a large number of victims with relatively limited logistical and organisational demands. It also aims to frighten and debilitate its victims by giving the impression that they are never truly safe. By targeting ordinary citizens rather than political figures, the Islamic State wants to show that we are in a way responsible for the decisions taken by our politicians, because they have been democratically elected and act in the name of the people.

In addition, many experts agree that ISIL also wants to encourage the conflation of Islam and terrorism. If the two become close enough in people's minds, this could lead to the rejection of the Muslim community; once abandoned by the West, these Muslims will be more easily won over by the caliphate's plans.

Shia Muslims are also targeted by ISIL because of their secular opposition in religious matters. The terrorist group also accuses them of having profited from the marginalisation of Sunnis following the American invasion in 2003, by occupying key positions in the administration. This means that, in a way, they are allies of the West.

STRATEGY

In order to achieve its aims, ISIL reportedly relies on a theoretical programme defined in part in a work entitled *Management of Savagery: The Most Critical Stage Through Which the Islamic Nation Will Pass* (2004), written by a member of al-Qaeda. This programme is made up of three phases. The first involves weakening the enemy through constant violence; in this way, the jihadists encourage chaos. The targeted population will gradually lose faith in its government. Once chaos has taken hold, the Islamic State will embark on the second phase of its plan, which involves winning the support of the people. To do this, it must establish itself as the only organisation capable of bringing a semblance of order to society. It will then need to re-establish security and put in place an aid system in order to offer food, healthcare, and so on to the suffering population. The last step in the plan is the proclamation of the caliphate.

HOW ISIL WORKS

AN EMBRYONIC STATE

Unlike other jihadist groups, the Islamic State is trying to set up a territorial base for itself. It is aware that its stability depends on efficient organisation and the effective management of the populations living under its authority.

The caliph, Abu Bakr al-Baghdadi, is at the head of the Islamic State. As the only leader of the Muslim community, he receives full power from God in the religious, political, judicial and military spheres. Around him is a government comprised of seven men, who are responsible for the supervision of prisoners, finances, coordination between the provinces, security, the welcoming of foreign combatants and military operations. Three members of the War Council are tasked with the management of vehicles and weapons, IED attacks, martyrs and women.

All those living in ISIL-controlled territories must submit to Islamic law (sharia), and the group has its own police force to ensure that this law is respected by the population. Its members can be recognised by their qamis, a sort of long tunic, sometimes worn with a black sleeveless jacket. Infractions are judged by Islamic courts, and the protection of the local population is ensured by civilian militants.

On 13 November 2014, the Islamic State announced the creation of its own currency, which probably entered circulation in June 2015. Although there is certainly a desire to move away from the Western and Jewish economic system, this is first and foremost a powerful symbol. Minting its own money is a sign of a state's power and independence. The gold and silver coins feature symbols of Islam and the Islamic State. They are dated from 1436 AH (*Anno Hegirae*, "in the year of the Hijra"; the Hijri year denotes the era beginning with the migration of Muhammad and his followers from Mecca to Medina), which corresponds to 2014 in the Gregorian calendar.

Al-Baghdadi is aware of the need to obtain the consent of the populations ISIL rules over in order to establish a modern state. This is achieved through social programmes. In addition, in its quest for new territories, the Islamic State particularly targets zones where there is a glaring lack of political authority. In this context, where economic matters take priority over political issues, it is enough to devote a small proportion of the budget to providing supplies for the population in order to ensure their support. The rest of the funds are then poured into military spending. According to some accounts, civilian militants organise soup kitchens to help those who have lost their homes, hand out bread and vegetables, produce uninterrupted electricity and improve the daily lives of Sunnis in the newly conquered territories. For example, the Islamic State has set up a body in Raqqa to find new families for orphaned children. Health programmes and polio vaccination programmes have also been set up. Furthermore, the Islamic State shares the resources it acquires as part of its conquests with the local populations. These populations can then benefit from the wealth they were denied by the Iraqi and Syrian political authorities.

In this way, al-Baghdadi applies a form of diplomacy by consensus, which proves very effective for making allies of the local Sunni communities and freeing the Islamic State from dependency on its foreign sponsors.

LIFE UNDER THE ISLAMIC STATE

Rules of life

Describing daily life for those living in territories occupied by ISIL is a particularly complex task, because little information is available and the sources we do have lack objectivity. The group maintains strict control over information and bans the use of cameras within the territories it controls, under pain of death. Conversely, the internet, which is often the only way individuals can contact their loved ones, is still allowed, although access to it is strictly controlled so that the Islamic State can preserve its stranglehold on information. Only its fighters can use the internet and film their daily lives without restrictions.

ISIL imposes very strict rules of life in an effort to go back to the message of the Qur'an as it was delivered by the Prophet. These rules are taught in schools as part of a curriculum designed by the Islamic State in order to win young people over to its cause. According to some sources, history lessons are limited to the life of Muhammad and the development of Islam. Most of the other human sciences have disappeared from the curriculum. Tobacco, alcohol, music and leisure activities are formally banned. Shops are closed in the afternoons, and the streets are completely deserted at nightfall. Anyone who disobeys the caliph risks extremely harsh punishments: execution by shooting, beheading or public mutilation, crucifixion, stoning and amputation, among others. Homosexuality, blasphemy, treason and adultery are all punishable by death.

Women are considered to be second-class citizens with no political rights, and their access to healthcare and education is restricted. They can only leave the family home if they are chaperoned by a male family member. Apart from their eyes, they must be covered from head to toe (including face and hands) by black clothing, in order to hide their bodies as much as possible.

Persecution of 'infidels'

According to the most radical Salafists, not subscribing to their religious ideology is such a grave sin that it merits death. This is why al-Baghdadi's men are carrying out a veritable ethnical cleansing of those they view as 'infidels', including Yazidis, Christians and Shia Muslims. When they are not forcibly converted, these religious communities are reduced to the rank of *dhimmis*, a lower status attributed to non-Muslims which forces them to pay an additional tax. This tax is supposed to protect them, but in reality it does not stop them from being violently attacked and murdered.

A mass grave of Yazidis in north-west Iraq.

As such, men, women and children from Shia communities are regularly massacred and have their houses looted and their mosques and sanctuaries destroyed. When they are kidnapped, the women and children are treated as chattels over which their owners have full rights: physical violence, prostitution, slavery, rape and forced marriage with members of ISIL are therefore common practice.

THE FINANCING OF ISLAMIC STATE

Foreign assistance

From 2003 onwards, several of the Gulf states, including Qatar and Saudi Arabia, and in particular Salafist circles, have provided financial support to the insurrection in Iraq. Thanks to these Gulf states, which are allies of the USA, the Islamic State has access to Western military technology. As part of the civil war in Syria, it has also been able to profit from arms provided to Bashar al-Assad by Russia, and to the opposition forces by America, by seizing them whenever the opportunity arises. In addition, the Sunni countries in the Middle East consider Tehran as an enemy because Iran is a powerful Shia country in the region. The wealthy Gulf states, where Salafism has deep roots, hope that, if Assad's regime is toppled, Iran will lose a valuable Shia ally.

THE ROLE OF BASHAR AL-ASSAD IN THE DEVELOPMENT OF THE ISLAMIC STATE

Bashar al-Assad is partly responsible for the development of the Islamic State. From 2011 onwards, he allowed jihadist networks to spread across his country in order to stem the movements protesting against his regime. Furthermore, when Western countries challenged his authoritarian leadership, he managed to join forces with them, as they would rather fight against terrorists who threaten the world order.

Turkey's position is very ambiguous. The Kurds, who have

a sizeable presence in Turkey, have been demanding their independence for a long time. It is therefore in the best interests of President Erdogan (born in 1954) to let the Islamic State oppress the Kurds. This is why the borders which Turkey shares with Syria and Iraq have for a long time remained porous, allowing men and arms to pass through.

These various countries, which have all contributed in one way or another to the emergence of the monster that is the Islamic State, risk paying a heavy price for their actions one day. In spite of the aid it has provided, ISIL views Saudi Arabia as a corrupt regime which has allied itself with the West, and for this reason believes that it must be destroyed. This prospect drove Saudi Arabia and nine other Arab countries to join the international coalition against the Islamic State. For its part, Turkey, which had for a long time turned a blind eye to what was happening along its borders, has fallen victim to a series of terrorist attacks.

Towards financial emancipation

Thanks to its territorial advances, a number of oilfields and gas extraction sites have fallen into the hands of the Islamic State, resulting in a sizeable financial windfall. As such, it was estimated in 2014 that the organisation was making $2 million per day through oil exports (in particular to Turkey), its primary source of revenue.

The conquest of territories also results in considerable war spoils, mainly thanks to the looting of banks. As such, when it seized the Central Bank in Mosul, the group acquired over $400 million. ISIL also profits from museums, which house extremely valuable archaeological treasures from the pre-Islamic age. These relics are often sold all over the world on the black market. Taxes and extortion bring in around $8 million per month. Slave trafficking and kidnappings in exchange for ransom money are another very profitable activity.

These various resources guarantee very comfortable financial prospects for the Islamic State. In 2014, the CIA estimated the size of its war chest at $2 billion. Thanks to money brought in by the sale of oil and extortion in its territory – estimated at $20 million in 2014 – it has gradually been able to free itself from its foreign sponsors and increase its independence.

AFFILIATIONS

Al-Qaeda

The Islamic State maintains a particular relationship with al-Qaeda. The group, which is a descendent of the Iraqi branch of Osama bin Laden's organisation, seems to want to rapidly gain the upper hand over its parent movement. On 9 April 2013, Abu Bakr al-Baghdadi announced that his organisation was joining with Jabhat al-Nusra (Victory Front), a group of Syrian jihadists fighting Bashar al-Assad's regime and constituting the Syrian branch of al-Qaeda. This resulted in the creation of the Islamic State of Iraq and the Levant. However, the emir of al-Nusra, Abu Mohammad al-Julani (born in 1981) refuted this alliance and reiterated the group's allegiance to al-Qaeda and its leader, Ayman al-Zawahiri.

It is true that, in spite of their ideological similarities, the al-Nusra fighters did not really support this alliance, as al-Baghdadi's combatants are not seeking freedom from Assad's tyranny. However, in addition, and perhaps most importantly, al-Baghdadi and his predecessors have always supported the fight of Sunni Arabs against Shia Muslims and Iran. Al-Qaeda sees a risk of disagreement between Muslims in this fight, and therefore prefers to focus its efforts on the struggle against the West and its allies in the Middle East.

There ensued a bloody internecine combat in Syria at the start of 2014. Al-Baghdadi's men ultimately triumphed over al-Nusra, and this victory enabled the Islamic State to take over a vast swathe of territory. As the group now controlled a number of oil wells, al-Baghdadi no longer needed the support of al-Qaeda and proclaimed his organisation's independence from the jihadist group.

Other groups

Although the Islamic State has established itself in Syria and Iraq, its influence extends far beyond these two countries. It has a number of affiliates in the Middle East and Africa, particularly in politically fragile areas. For example, the organisation has been taking advantage of the instability that has prevailed in Libya since the fall of Muammar Gadhafi (1942-2011) in 2011. The situation is similar in Egypt and Algeria, which have both aligned themselves with the caliphate. In Saudi Arabia, a group called Wilayat Najd has been carrying out terrorist attacks with the aim of destabilising the government.

However, the most powerful group to have sworn allegiance to the Islamic State is undeniably Boko Haram, led by Abubakar Shekau (born between 1965 and 1975). It sows terror in northern Nigeria and Cameroon, the area around Lake Chad and south-east Niger.

Two men lie wounded following an attack by Boko Haram in 2014.

Other organisations which support the Islamic State ensure that the organisation has a presence in Southeast Asia and Bangladesh, regions where Islam has deep roots.

Globally, the Islamic State is affiliated with groups establi-shed in the entire northern half of Africa, in Somalia and across the entire Middle East (with the exception of the Sultanate of Oman), in the region stretching from Turkey to Pakistan, as well as in Bangladesh and Southeast Asia.

RECRUITMENT AND COMMUNICATION STRATEGIES

Mediums of communication

The propaganda developed by the Islamic State has two aims: to recruit new members and to terrorise its enemies. To do this, the group has developed an extremely effective communication strategy. Its communication service, al-Hayat Media Center, publishes many written, audio and video messages. The group also has its own information agency, A'amaq ("Depths" in English), which publishes information about the Islamic State, its battles and speeches delivered by its leaders online. Its online magazine *Dabiq* (named after the Syrian town captured by the Islamic State in 2014, and a prophetic location where the organisation believes that the final battle between Muslim and infidel forces will take place) has been published since 2014. It features interviews with hostages, calls to join the lands of the caliphate, calls to jihad and articles which aim to justify the decisions of the group's leaders.

A service called al-Furqan (named after the 25th sura of the Qur'an) is responsible for the production and distribution of propaganda videos. The films it produces are greatly inspired by Hollywood standards: they are always carefully directed with the aim of drawing in the viewer, while depicting extreme violence in order to accustom viewers to brutality. They showcase figures who are depicted as heroes that young people can identify with.

Whatever form they take, the messages of ISIL propaganda

are always the same. They demonstrate a very black-and-white, simplistic view of the world, in which the West and its allies persecute Muslims and are therefore blamed for the decline of Islam. According to the group, the only way of putting an end to this state of affairs is to join the caliphate, the only guardian of the Truth, and to annihilate the enemy, which it presents as totally dehumanised. The Islamic State promises its fighters that they will be rewarded with life in heaven after death. This life will be eternal and far better than our earthly existence. This indoctrination allows the group to turn its members into killing machines who do not fear death.

The Islamic State also cultivates a sense of mystery in order to touch the collective imagination and stir people's curiosity and imagination. This approach is all the more effective given that Islam is a religion based on the mystery of the return of Muhammad. The Islamic State's propaganda apparatus makes great use of this expectation to construct a sort of mythology around the caliphate and al-Baghdadi, who, according to them, embodies in a way the return of the Prophet. Moreover, there are only two known photographs of al-Baghdadi prior to the proclamation of the caliphate.

One of the two confirmed photographs of Abu Bakr al-Baghdadi.

The manipulation of the media and social networks

After they are posted online, messages, videos and other content spread across the world, in particular thanks to social networks, which are used by huge numbers of young people. From 2011 onwards, an online propaganda campaign sought to make audiences believe that ISIL was incredibly strong, when in reality it was on the brink of extinction. This approached proved highly effective: experienced fighters, in particular from Bosnia and Chechnya, joined its ranks and helped to boost the strength of its army. This strategy is still used today. A potential jihadist will always prefer to join a successful group than a movement that is struggling to establish itself.

The Islamic State is also increasingly prominent on Twitter, where it has its own news feed. It also seizes the opportunity to leverage global events to expand its potential audience. For example, during the 2014 World Cup, members of ISIL used hashtags such as #Brazil2014, #ENG and #WC2014 in their tweets so that they would appear in searches related to the World Cup. By clicking on the links, Twitter users would then be directed to propaganda messages calling for jihad.

The Islamic State also manipulates the traditional press through the shocking images it publishes, since if the press chooses not to broadcast these images, it risks failing to cover some current affairs and losing some of its audience. In addition, the media only has access to documents distributed by the Islamic State itself, as journalists on the ground are often kidnapped and executed by al-Baghdadi's men. The group's strategy thus involves using exceptionally violent images as a way of displaying its power and exploiting people's fears, which is a formidably effective weapon.

Recruitment cells

Although some experts prefer not to put forward a typical profile of the kind of person who is likely to join the Islamic State, it is possible to outline a number of traits shared by recruits.

In a world facing economic, political and philosophical crisis, ISIL targets young people who are looking for a sense of identity, are worried about their future and sometimes feel a profound sense of failure. These young people often have little formal education and know next to nothing about Islam. As they lack critical thinking skills, they are easily won over by charismatic Salafists and self-proclaimed imams who transmit the Islamic State's ideology on the ground. They take advantage of the struggles of these disaffected young people and try to persuade them that their problems are linked to the Western lifestyle and to Westerners' racism against Arabs.

By joining the caliphate and taking part in jihad, young people are offered a real purpose, not only on Earth, but also after their death. In this way, they hope to receive a form of recognition for their existence by becoming heroes of Islam, or even martyrs. The Islamic State tells them that they are certain to reach paradise and that the men among them will be rewarded with 72 virgins. In addition, Islamists present becoming a martyr as the only way of atoning for one's sins, whereas in reality Islam offers a range of other paths to redemption, starting with Ramadan. To convince potential new members, recruiters use a very radical, and often distorted, interpretation of some verses of the Qur'an that have been removed from their historical context.

THE FIGHT AGAINST THE ISLAMIC STATE

THE ARMED CONFLICT IN SYRIA: GEOPOLITICS AND A PROXY WAR

Although Barack Obama (former president of the USA, born in 1961) initially did not want to get involved in conflicts in the Middle East, he changed his position in summer 2014 when he decided to use force to fight against jihadists in Iraq. He feared that the Islamic State would expand and permanently establish itself in the region, which would threaten American interests in the Middle East. This change in position came about following the beheading of the American journalist James Foley close to Raqqa on 19 August 2014. On 10 September of that year, Obama announced his intention to form an international coalition under the auspices of NATO and to launch an aerial bombardment campaign over Syria in order to destroy the caliphate. An initial coalition brought together some 30 countries, including the five permanent members of the United Nations Security Council (China, France, Russia, the UK and the USA) and around ten Arab countries (in particular Saudi Arabia, Qatar, Jordan, Bahrain and the United Arab Emirates). The aim was to fight the presence of ISIL in Iraq, in particular by supporting the Iraqi government in its fight. Australia, Belgium, Denmark and Germany later joined the coalition.

US Army paratroopers, part of the coalition forces, in training in Iraq, 2015.

However, no country wanted to send in troops on the ground for fear of getting stuck in a quagmire like the one in Afghanistan. The Western countries that had joined the coalition favoured aerial bombardments. They also lent their support to local armed groups opposed to ISIL, thus embarking on a proxy war. With this in mind, the White House gave over $500 million so that a largely secular opposition force, opposed to both the Islamic State and Bashar al-Assad, could be set up in Syria. The combatants who joined this force had mainly been trained by Iran, a Shia country which aimed to support the Iraqi leaders by fighting against local Sunni powers. However, the effectiveness of this tactic proved limited, as a collection of small organisations was no match for an army as powerful as that of the Islamic State.

The groups which took up arms against ISIL include the Kurdistan Workers' Party (PKK), which received support from the USA in August 2014. Now, however, this organisation is officially recognised by Washington as a terrorist group. It is also historically an enemy of Turkey. As Ankara had joined the international coalition against the Islamic State, geopolitical issues led the PPK to fight alongside it. Other groups were also supported by the Gulf states in their fight against the Islamist monster they had helped to create. The problem for the West was that these groups were Salafists or close to the Muslim Brotherhood, such as the Army of Mujahideen, which wanted to put in place a Muslim regime in Syria.

Bashar al-Assad and his main ally Vladimir Putin (president of Russia, born in 1952) have also made the West's fight against Daesh more difficult. Although he wanted to fight resolutely against the Islamic State, the Syrian president categorially refused to permit any air strike by the USA against the group. This severely complicated the White House's plans, as sending planes to Syria would amount to attacking a UN member and would further jeopardise the country's already tense relations with Russia. However, Article 51 of the United Nations Charter authorises armed intervention in another country for reasons of self-defence.

China was also troubled by the situation in the Middle East. It feared a contagion effect in the autonomous region of Xinjiang, especially given that the country had faced several attacks since August 2013. It economic interests were also threatened, as 8% of the petrol it consumed came from

Iraq, and its presence in Africa was endangered, in particular by Boko Haram. This is why Beijing mainly deployed its army in Africa.

The efforts of the international community seem to have paid off. By the end of June 2016, the Islamic State had lost 45% of the territory it had conquered in Iraq, as well as Fallujah, the last bastion occupied by ISIL in Al Anbar, the main province in the country. The oil-rich lands around Kirkuk in northern Iraq were retaken by the Kurds in spring 2016. In Syria, Raqqa is currently the only major city held by al-Baghdadi. Its position has been under threat since the retaking of Palmyra by Syrian troops, and Kurdish and Arab troops are gradually approaching the city from the north. Furthermore, in June 2016 these troops seized the last road connecting the city with Turkey and which allowed large quantities of arms, goods and men to be transported via the black market.

As such, the Islamic State no longer controls the resources that ensured its financial security. This situation is exacerbated by the fact that the group has repeatedly turned against its various backers (al-Qaeda and the Gulf states).

In spite of the progress made by the international coalition, peace is still a long way off. The Iraqi government does not seem to be in a position to ensure the security and stability of the territories liberated from the Islamic State, where Sunni populations are still brutalised by Shia militias. Once the organisation has been defeated, it will be imperative to put in place a government that represents the different communities, not only to rebuild the ruined towns and cities, but also to ensure the control and security of the territory as a whole.

Counterpropaganda

Armed fighting in Islamic State territory will not be enough to defeat the organisation. Efforts are also being made to fight against jihadist propaganda on the internet in order to limit the number of new recruits. However, this combat is proving particularly difficult. Every time social networks close down accounts, new ones spring up in their place, limiting the effectiveness of this approach.

At the same time, many countries have embarked on counterpropaganda campaigns. For example, British community managers track all messages from the Islamic State on social media to counter their arguments, France has set up a website to warn against the dangers of jihadist terrorism and interpret propaganda messages, and the Center for Strategic Counterterrorism Communications in the USA broadcasts videos denouncing the Islamic State's extreme violence. However, at this stage it is still too early to judge their effectiveness.

THE VICTIMS OF THE ISLAMIC STATE

The various ethnic communities that make up Syria and Iraq are persecuted on a daily basis. This persecution particularly affects Shia Muslims and Eastern Christians. The many Sunnis who do not subscribe to ISIL's ideology and refuse to submit to al-Baghdadi are also persecuted. Because of the torture, persecution and rape carried out by the Islamic

State, the UN has accused the organisation of crimes against humanity.

This has resulted in mass migration towards Europe, the likes of which has not been seen since the Second World War (1939-1945). As well as being financially costly, these journeys are also very dangerous. After risking their lives crossing warzones and tightly controlled borders, hundreds of refugees pile into small boats to cross the Mediterranean, where shipwrecks are a common occurrence. For example, in September 2015, 2700 migrants died during their exodus. Their ordeal is not over once they set foot in Europe: they are left facing countries which refuse to welcome them or grant them asylum, as is the case in Austria and Hungary, in spite of the obligations imposed by the European Union.

Migrants crossing the border between Serbia and Hungary.

In addition to the populations who have been directly affected by ISIL, the Muslim community as a whole can also be counted among its victims, as many people are now quick to conflate them with extremists. By taking certain passages from the Qur'an out of context, Daesh gives a false vision of this sacred text, which those who are unfamiliar with the religion may take at face value. Through these actions, the Islamic State encourages the development and spread of racism, to the point that the integration of the Muslim community in Western societies has become particularly challenging. We cannot forget that racism towards Muslims in our countries results in a particularly fertile breeding ground for extremism.

SUMMARY

- The Islamic State of Iraq and the Levant emerged from a very heterogenous society marked by political interference. It has taken advantage of the marginalisation of some sectors of the population to considerably exacerbate cultural differences and stir up hatred between different groups. The development of the terrorist group also owes much to political issues in the Middle East and to the historical conflict between Sunnis and Shias.
- The leader of the Islamic State, Abu Bakr al-Baghdadi, is motivated by a desire to restore what he sees as the golden age of Islam by establishing a caliphate. He has proclaimed himself the leader of this caliphate, and seeks to apply sharia within it.
- The Islamic State has made the most of the drifting of a society in crisis: it appeals to disaffected young men to swell the ranks of its army, inviting them to wage jihad by promising them a purpose in life and a sure passage to heaven after their deaths. The group is prepared to embrace anyone who subscribes to its Salafist ideology. Conversely, it is ruthless towards those it considers to be 'infidels', who it views as deserving only death.
- Whatever its targets, the Islamic State's message is based on the idea that Muslims are victims, held in contempt by the West and its corrupt allies. It uses some extracts from the Qur'an, taken out of their historical context and given an extremely radical interpretation, to legitimise its message.
- The Islamic State takes a very pragmatic approach in

the dissemination of its propaganda messages and recruitment of new members, relying on a highly effective communication strategy. By employing extreme violence, which it makes visible through videos or images of executions, it relies on fear and manipulates the media, which is forced to broadcast its images if it wants to report on the group.

- The Islamic State tries to make allies of the population in its conquered territories in order to become a real state. It does this by ensuring that living conditions for Sunni populations within the caliphate improve.

- Due to the many strategic issues in the Middle East, a range of global forces and powers, often with very different and even diametrically opposed interests, have formed an alliance to combat this shared enemy. This geopolitical upheaval means that the fight against ISIL is not a classic war with two sides, but a many-sided conflict. This distinctive feature considerably complicates the task of setting up a united, effective coalition to overcome the Islamic State.

- In addition to the countless civilian victims who have lost their lives during the fighting or in terrorist attacks across the world, tens of thousands of people have left behind everything they have to flee from war and the oppression of ISIL. They risk their lives to reach Europe, which they see as a land of welcome and asylum. Furthermore, the Islamic State has played a major part in the development of the racism in the West towards the Muslim community. Through this approach, it hopes to turn Muslims away from the Western world and encourage them to join the terrorist group.

We want to hear from you!
Leave a comment on your online library
and share your favourite books on social media!

FIND OUT MORE

BIBLIOGRAPHY

- Amghar, S. (2015) Qu'est-ce que le salafisme ? *Sciences Humaines*. [Online]. [Accessed 21 March 2017]. Available from: <https://www.scienceshumaines.com/qu-est-ce-que-le-salafisme_fr_35302.html>
- Association France Press. (2015) Le chef du groupe EI en Libye tué par une frappe américaine. *La Libre Belgique*. [Online]. [Accessed 21 March 2017]. Available from: <http://www.lalibre.be/actu/international/le-chef-du-groupe-ei-en-libye-tue-par-une-frappe-americaine-564798223570bccfaf08e447>
- Bauchard, D. (2014) Le Moyen-Orient face à Daech. Défis et ripostes. *Institut français des relations internationales*. [Online]. [Accessed 21 March 2017]. Available from: <https://www.ifri.org/sites/default/files/atoms/files/bauchard-daech.pdf>
- Baudet, M-B. (2015) Sur la route des djihadistes, entre Anvers et Bruxelles. *Le Monde*. [Online]. [Accessed 21 March 2017]. Available from: <http://www.lemonde.fr/europe/article/2015/11/23/sur-la-route-des-djihadistes-entre-anvers-et-bruxelles_4815513_3214.html>
- Benkirane, R. (2015) Daech, un monstre que l'Occident a rendu possible. *Le Temps*. [Online]. [Accessed 21 March 2017]. Available from: <https://www.letemps.ch/opinions/2015/04/27/daech-un-monstre-occident-rendu-possible>
- Benraad, M. (2014) Les sunnites, l'Iraq et l'État islamique. *Esprit*, issue 11.

- Benraad, M. (2015) *Irak, la revanche de l'histoire : de l'occupation étrangère à l'État islamique*. Paris: Éditions Vendémiaire.
- Boniface, P. (2016) Quelle réponse face à menace terroriste ? *Institut de Relations Internationales et Stratégiques*. [Online]. [Accessed 21 March 2017]. Available from: <http://www.iris-france.org/73652-quelle-reponse-face-a-la-menace-terroriste/>
- Braun, V. (2015) Arabie saoudite : des hommages et des sabres. *La Libre Belgique*. [Online]. [Accessed 21 March 2017]. Available from: <http://www.lalibre.be/actu/international/arabie-saoudite-des-hommages-et-des-sabres-54c8065935700d75223e30b2>
- Braun, V. (2015) Un manque de respect nommé blaspheme. *La Libre Belgique*. [Online]. [Accessed 21 March 2017]. Available from: <http://www.lalibre.be/actu/international/un-manque-de-respect-nomme-blaspheme-54d50f0835701001a1963240>
- Braun, V. and Lamfalussy, C. (2016) Les deux fronts qui vont déstabiliser l'Etat islamique. *La Libre Belgique*. [Online]. [Accessed 21 March 2017]. Available from: <http://www.lalibre.be/actu/international/les-deux-fronts-qui-vont-destabiliser-l-etat-islamique-5746036035708ea2d5d77073>
- Duby, G. (2007) *Atlas historique mondial*. Paris: Larousse.
- Fellous, G. (2015) *Daech – « État islamique ». Cancer d'un monde arabo-musulman en recomposition. Un conflit international long et incertain*. Paris: Éditions L'Harmattan.
- Gambhir, H. (2016) ISIS Global Strategy: March 2016. *Institute for the Study of War*. [Online]. [Accessed

21 March 2017]. Available from: <http://understandingwar.org/map/isis-global-strategy-march-2016>

- Gambhir, H. (2016) ISIS-linked Activity in Southeast Asia: March 2 to April 21, 2016. *Institute for the Study of War.* [Online]. [Accessed 21 March 2017]. Available from: <http://www.understandingwar.org/backgrounder/isis-linked-activity-southeast-asia-march-2-april-21-2016>
- Human Rights Watch. (2016) *Iraq: Women Suffer Under ISIS.* [Online]. [Accessed 21 March 2017]. Available from: <https://www.hrw.org/news/2016/04/05/iraq-women-suffer-under-isis>
- Hussein, H. (2016) Comment l'« Etat islamique » détourne des textes et des codes islamiques pour se rendre plus attractif. *Les Cahiers d'Islam : Revue d'Études sur l'Islam et le Monde Musulman.* [Online]. [Accessed 21 March 2017]. Available from: <http://www.lescahiersdelislam.fr/Comment-l-Etat-islamique-detourne-des-textes-et-des-codes-islamiques-pour-se-rendre-plus-attractif_a1234.html>
- Hussein, H (2016) Les illusions de la propagande numérique de L' « Etat islamique ». *Les Cahiers d'Islam : Revue d'Études sur l'Islam et le Monde Musulman.* [Online]. [Accessed 21 March 2017]. Available from: <http://www.lescahiersdelislam.fr/Les-illusions-de-la-propagande-numerique-de-L-Etat-islamique_a1252.html>
- Hussein, H. and al-Ajamî, M. (2016) Le djihad fantasmé de Daesh. *Contre-discours radical.* [Online]. [Accessed 21 March 2017]. Available from: <https://cdradical.hypotheses.org/15>
- Institut de Relations Internationales et Stratégiques. (No date) *Homepage.* [Online]. [Accessed 21 March 2017].

Available from: <http://www.iris-france.org/>

- Institute for the Study of War. (2016) *ISIS's Regional Campaign: April 2016.* [Online]. [Accessed 21 March 2017]. Available from: <http://understandingwar.org/map/isiss-regional-campaign-april-2016>
- Institute for the Study of War. (No date) *Homepage.* [Online]. [Accessed 21 March 2017]. Available from: <http://understandingwar.org/>
- Jambu, J. (2016) Quand Daech frappe sa monnaie. *L'Histoire*, issue 421, pp. 18-19.
- Karouny, M. (2014) Life under Isis: For residents of Raqqa is this really a caliphate worse than death? *The Independent.* [Online]. [Accessed 21 March 2017]. Available from: <http://www.independent.co.uk/news/world/middle-east/life-under-isis-for-residents-of-raqqa-is-this-really-a-caliphate-worse-than-death-9715799.html>
- Lamfalussy, C. (2016) Daech perd le contrôle de son axe vers la Turquie. *La Libre Belgique.* [Online]. [Accessed 21 March 2017]. Available from: <http://www.lalibre.be/actu/international/daech-perd-le-controle-de-son-axe-vers-la-turquie-5754483235708ea2d62f9b34>
- Larousse. (No date) *Iraq : histoire.* [Online]. [Accessed 21 March 2017]. Available from: <http://www.larousse.fr/encyclopedie/divers/%20%20Iraq%20_%20histoire/187631>
- Les Cahiers de l'Islam: Revue d'Études sur l'Islam et le Monde Musulman. (No date) *Homepage.* [Online]. [Accessed 21 March 2017]. Available from: <http://www.lescahiersdelislam.fr/>
- Le Vif. (2015) *Al-Zarquaoui, le délinquant à l'origine de*

Daech. [Online]. [Accessed 21 March 2017]. Available from: <http://www.levif.be/actualite/international/al-zarqaoui-le-delinquant-a-l-origine-de-daech/article-normal-408653.html>

- L'Histoire. (2016) *Le vrai pouvoir des califes.* Issue 423, pp. 42-65.
- Mediapart. (2015) *Le management de la sauvagerie, l'étape la plus critique que franchira l'oumma.* [Online]. [Accessed 21 March 2017]. Available from: <https://blogs.mediapart.fr/danyves/blog/150615/le-management-de-la-sauvagerie-l-etape-la-plus-critique-que-franchira-l-oumma>
- Mohsin, M. (2016) De la délinquance à l'extrémisme. *La Libre Belgique.* [Online]. [Accessed 21 March 2017]. Available from: <http://www.lalibre.be/debats/opinions/de-la-delinquance-a-l-extremisme-570e6bf-f35708ea2d4818fca>
- Napoleoni, L. (2015) *L'État islamique : multinationale de la violence.* Paris: Calmann-Lévy.
- Pakzad, K. (2016) Constituer une coalition pour défaire l'État islamique : quels enjeux, quelles conséquences ? *Institut de Relations Internationales et Stratégiques.* [Online]. [Accessed 21 March 2017]. Available from: <http://www.iris-france.org/43907-constituer-une-coalition-pour-defaire-letat-islamique-quels-enjeux-quelles-consequences/>
- Pakzad, K. (2016) Irak : où en est la situation politique et militaire ? *Institut de Relations Internationales et Stratégiques.* [Online]. [Accessed 21 March 2017]. Available from: <http://www.iris-france.org/73866-irak-ou-en-est-la-situation-politique-et-militaire/>

- Plummer, W. (2016) Face à Daech, qui fait quoi dans la coalition… pour quels résultats ? *Le Figaro*. [Online]. [Accessed 21 March 2017]. Available from: <http://www.lefigaro.fr/international/2016/01/08/01003-20160108ARTFIG00011-face-a-daech-qui-fait-quoi-pour-quels-resultats.php>
- Revue Hérotode. (2016) *Le monde arabe, regards géopolitiques*. Issues 160-161.
- Roy, O. (2015) Le djihadisme est une révolte générationnelle et nihiliste. *Le Monde*. [Online]. [Accessed 21 March 2017]. Available from: <http://www.lemonde.fr/idees/article/2015/11/24/le-djihadisme-une-revolte-generationnelle-et-nihiliste_4815992_3232.html>
- Sourdel, J. and Sourdel, D. (1996) *Dictionnaire historique de l'islam*. Paris: Presses universitaires de France.
- Stop-djihadisme.gouv.fr (No date) *Homepage*. [Online]. [Accessed 21 March 2017]. Available from: <http://www.stop-djihadisme.gouv.fr/>
- US Department of State Diplomacy in Action. (2015) *Country Reports on Terrorism 2014*. [Online]. [Accessed 21 March 2017]. Available from: <https://www.state.gov/j/ct/rls/crt/2014/index.htm>
- Van de Woestyne, F. (2015) Détourner le regard de cette photo, c'est se détourner du drame. *La Libre Belgique*. [Online]. [Accessed 21 March 2017]. Available from: <http://www.lalibre.be/debats/edito/edito-detourner-le-regard-de-cette-photo-c-est-se-detourner-du-drame-55e88f423570ebab3d82128e>
- Vaudano, M. (2014) Quelles sont les différences entre sunnites et chiites ? *Le Monde*. [Online]. [Accessed 21 March 2017]. Available from: <http://www.lemonde.

- fr/les-decodeurs/article/2014/06/20/au-fait-quelle-difference-entre-sunnites-et-chiites_4442319_4355770.html>
- Vernier, E. (2015) Veut-on vraiment s'attaquer aux finances de l'État islamique ? *Institut de Relations Internationales et Stratégiques.* [Online]. [Accessed 21 March 2017]. Available from: <http://www.iris-france.org/66829-veut-on-vraiment-sattaquer-aux-finances-de-letat-islamique/>
- Verhest, S. (2015) Voici comment se finance l'Etat islamique. *La Libre Belgique.* [Online]. [Accessed 21 March 2017]. Available from: <http://www.lalibre.be/actu/international/voici-comment-se-finance-l-etat-isla-mique-564769f33570bccfaf07c4b8>
- Zerrouky, M. (2016) Qu'apprend-on aux enfants à l'école de l'Etat islamique. *Le Monde.* [Online]. [Accessed 21 March 2017]. Available from: <http://www.lemonde.fr/international/article/2016/04/22/a-l-ecole-de-l-etat-islamique_4907106_3210.html>

ADDITIONAL SOURCES

- Atwan, A-B. (2015) *Islamic State: The Digital Caliphate.* London: Saqi Books.
- Cockburn, P. (2015) *The Rise of Islamic State: ISIS and the New Sunni Revolution.* London: Verso.
- Kilcullen, D. (2016) *Blood Year: Islamic State and the Failures of the War on Terror.* London: C. Hurst & Co.
- Napoleoni, L. (2014) *The Islamic Phoenix: The Islamic State and the Redrawing of the Middle East.* New York: Seven Stories Press.

- Napoleoni, L. (2017) *ISIS: The Terror Nation*. New York: Seven Stories Press.
- Napoleoni, L. (2017) *Merchants of Men: How Kidnapping, Ransom and Trafficking Funds Terrorism and ISIS*. London: Atlantic Books.
- Stern, J. and Berger, J. M. (2016) *ISIS: The State of Terror*. New York: HarperCollins.
- Warrick, J. (2016) *Black Flags: The Rise of ISIS*. London: Corgi.
- Wood, G. (2016) *The Way of the Strangers: Encounters with the Islamic State*. London: Penguin.

ICONOGRAPHIC SOURCES

- The flag of the Islamic State. Royalty-free reproduction picture.
- The al-Assad family: Hafez al-Assad and his wife (seated); behind him are his children, including Bashar al-Assad (second from left). Royalty-free reproduction picture.
- Photograph of Saddam Hussein. Royalty-free reproduction picture.
- Photograph taken in 2004 in Fallujah, a city in central Iraq which became the scene of violence clashes. © US Marine Corps.
- The UN headquarters in Baghdad after a truck bombing in August 2013. Royalty-free reproduction picture.
- A mass grave of Yazidis in north-west Iraq. © Êzîdî Press.
- Two men lie wounded following an attack by Boko Haram in 2014. Royalty-free reproduction picture.
- One of the two confirmed photographs of Abu Bakr

al-Baghdadi. © US Army.
- US Army paratroopers, part of the coalition forces, in training in Iraq, 2015. Royalty-free reproduction picture.
- Migrants crossing the border between Serbia and Hungary. © Gémes Sándor.

DOCUMENTARIES

- *The Islamic State.* (2014) [Documentary]. Medyan Dairieh. Dir. USA: VICE News.
- *I Want to Live.* (2015) [Documentary]. Karzan Kardozi. Dir. Iraq/Syria/Iran.
- *Life Inside 'Islamic State'.* (2017) [Documentary]. Scott Coello. Dir. United Kingdom: British Broadcasting Company.

IMPROVE YOUR GENERAL KNOWLEDGE

IN A BLINK OF AN EYE !

www.50minutes.com